# PEARL

# Pearl

Poems by Vincent Katz

Paintings by Tabboo!

powerHouse Books
NEW YORK, NY

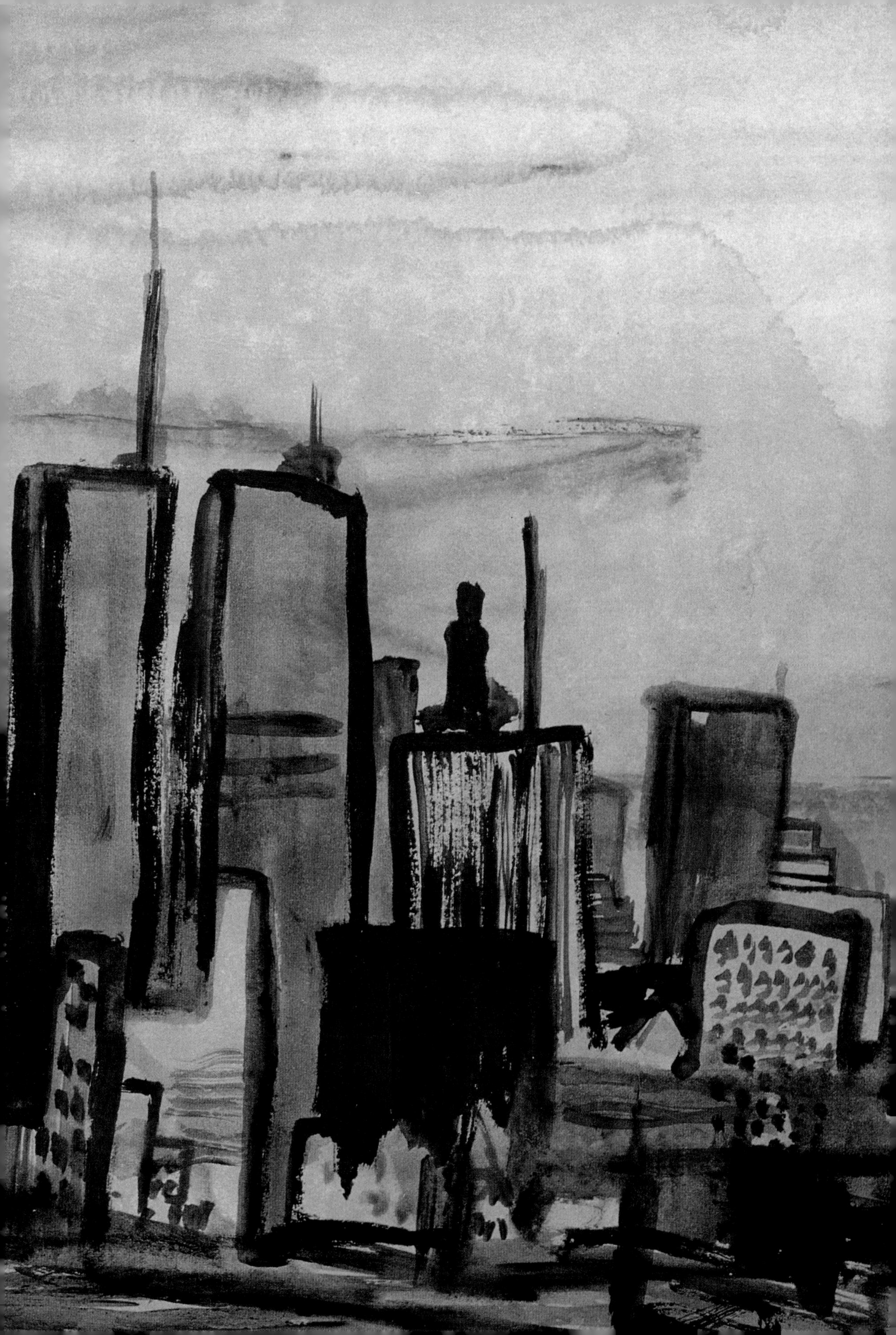

ἐπίσταμαι δὲ τοσοῦτον ὅτι εἰ
πάντες ἄνθρωποι τὰ οἰκήια κακὰ
ἐς μέσον συνενείκαιεν ἀλλάξασθαι
βουλόμενοι τοῖσι πλησίοισι,
ἐγκύψαντες ἂν ἐς τὰ τῶν
πέλας κακὰ ἀσπασίως ἕκαστοι
αὐτῶν ἀποφεροίατο ὀπίσω τὰ
ἐσηνείκαντο.

I really believe that if everybody were to bring all their problems together, with the idea of trading theirs with other people's—once they'd had a good, long look at everybody else's, they would all gladly take their own back home.

Herodotos (vii.152)

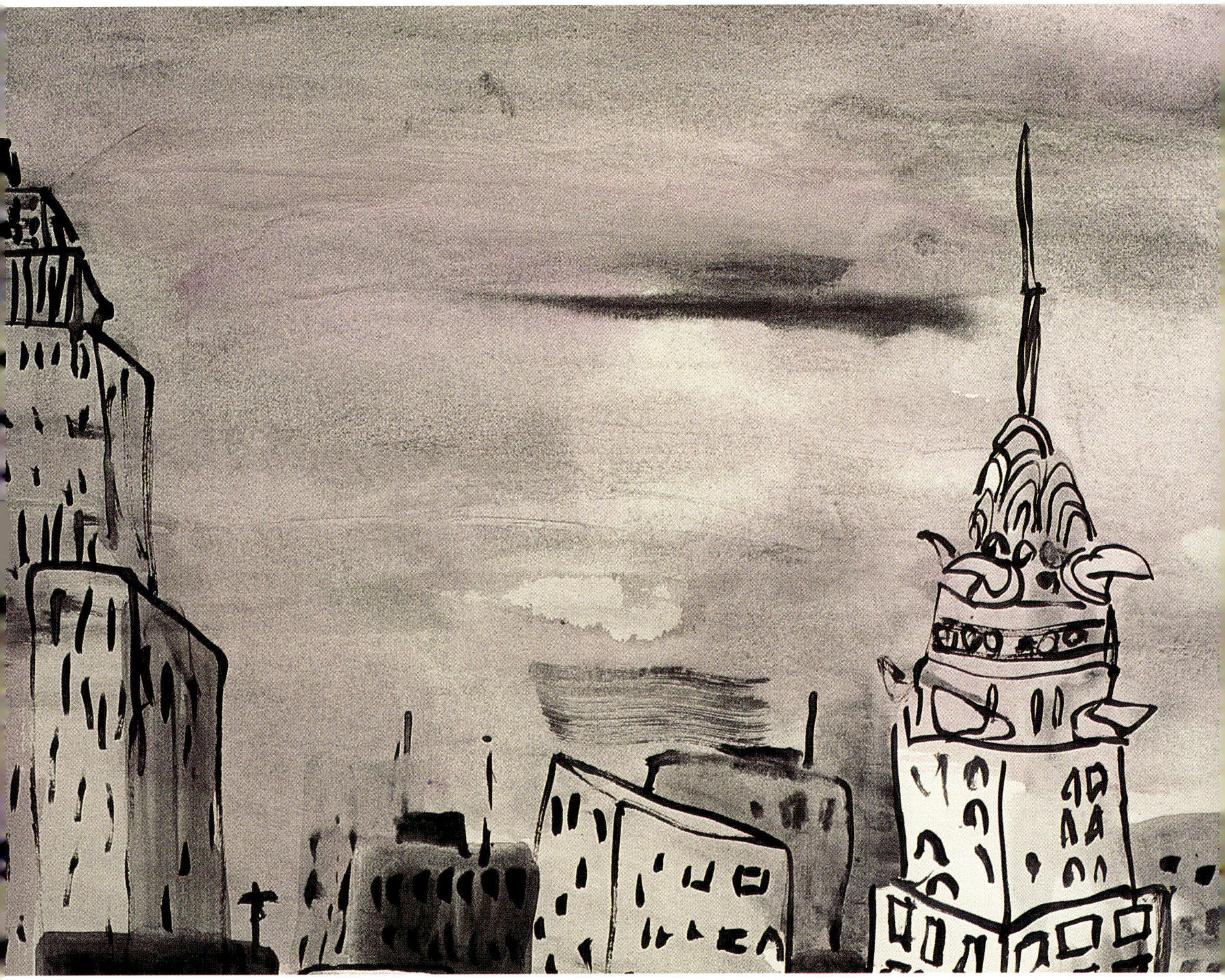

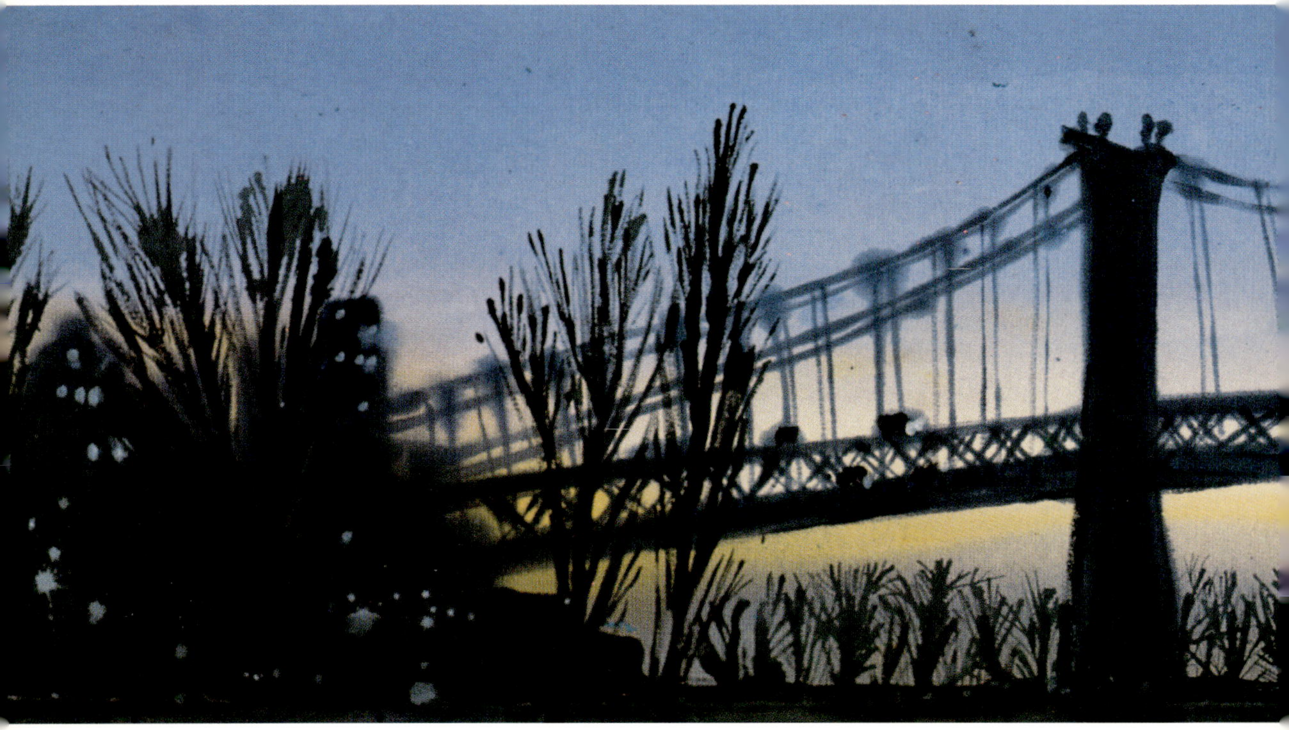

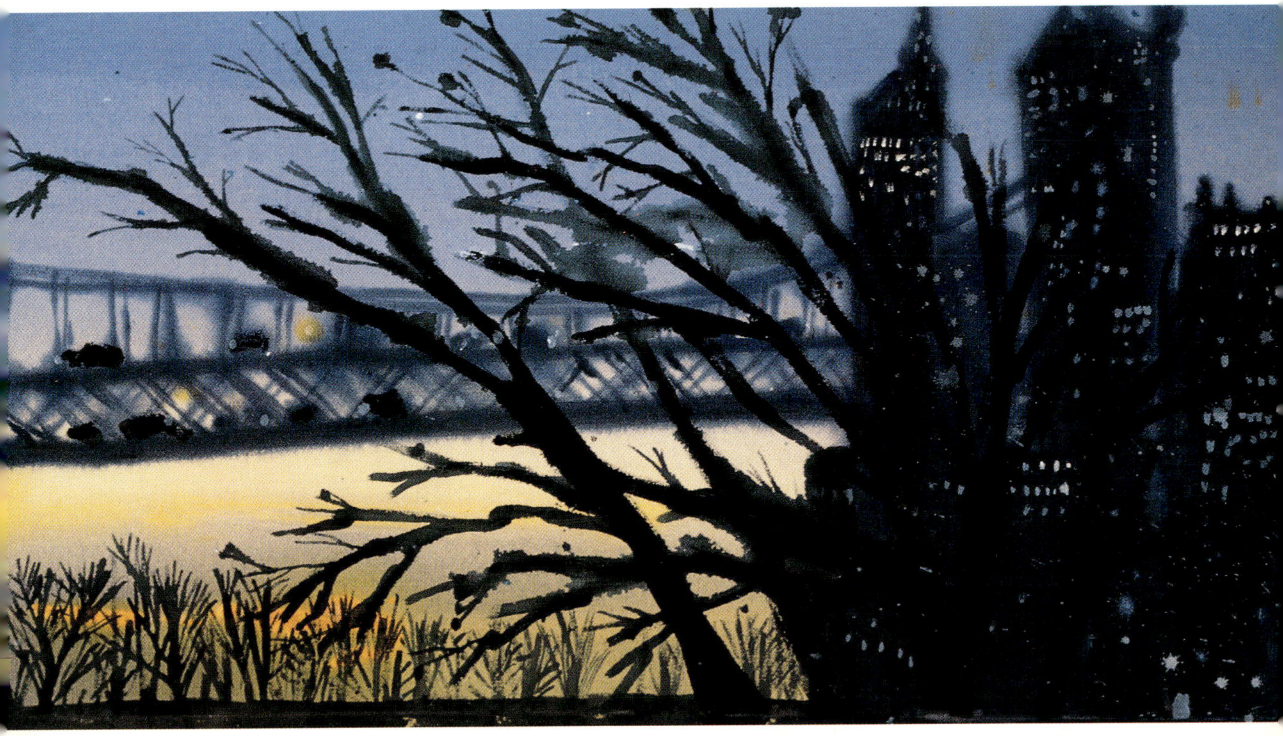

Kept crawling to Happy Mondays
scalp infested by hundred-fingered
ants, slow flying moths
Heavy D's in effec'
olivetti freeze-frame of Homosexuality
a bridge of Chicago, what is
happening to nature? it's disappearing
shower-headed lust, chance

*

## alba's roach

alba left a roach and I got it:
perfumed sardanopolos in flames of decay,
hunched abandon over a web of ways,
ideas that had fluttered as hand
on glass of wine, there is very little
value in defining anything, a flower
rose from my breast and I planted it
there, where francesco had seen the suitcase
dripping blood; conceivably the host
had planned for these shortcomings,
a dreadful blast that had shuddered
near muntins of blessed deceit, the way
the fingers of her hand respond.

but there's more: a perfumed ecstasy
I couldn't hold, till the guests had all
turned to cold night, it was like the smell
of a situation, a society, concurring
in a rapidly diminishing fire of pipes.

a new day hath dawned
alba's roach is gone

*

## Big Red

the team is a beautiful thing
I shoot the Midwest between my legs
the temple of her body is violated

*

"We often forget that each unit in the mass is a
        throbbing human soul."
                        —W. E. B. DuBois

*

Come, fill the bucket
    drain the dregs
Put your butt to the saddle
    the day is old enough
        to beg
sick of this bullshit head.

*

that's the real version as far as I'm concerned
the real dick in the ass of taste

*

And yet, if I have failure imprinted
on my soul, perhaps this is still
a way to achieve my fatalistic ends.

We know where you live:
Truth, Justice, and the Comics.

I am become a Technician

*

## a Morganic experience

*Perhaps you and I*
*should just fly*
*in a pixilated sky*

*The window disappears*
*back into the disk icon.*

Rudy had been feeling something
in his eye, so we tried
a brownie you had given me
3 months by—Mamoun it was
you called it, with molasses, nuts,
and herb. Then blank frames
intersected us, yellow tulips
glowed dazily, we went through
streets to a church. I'm
always nervous in the church
but there are lots of echoes there
I heard. Then the play
began. We saw bright
reflections on the floor,
and our friends entered,
one by one. Rosemary is
so elegant in her pregnant
pink cape! And Roberta
resolutely sexy. Then we
were walking and seeing
vast flashes in New York's
firmament, underneath
its most beautiful monuments—

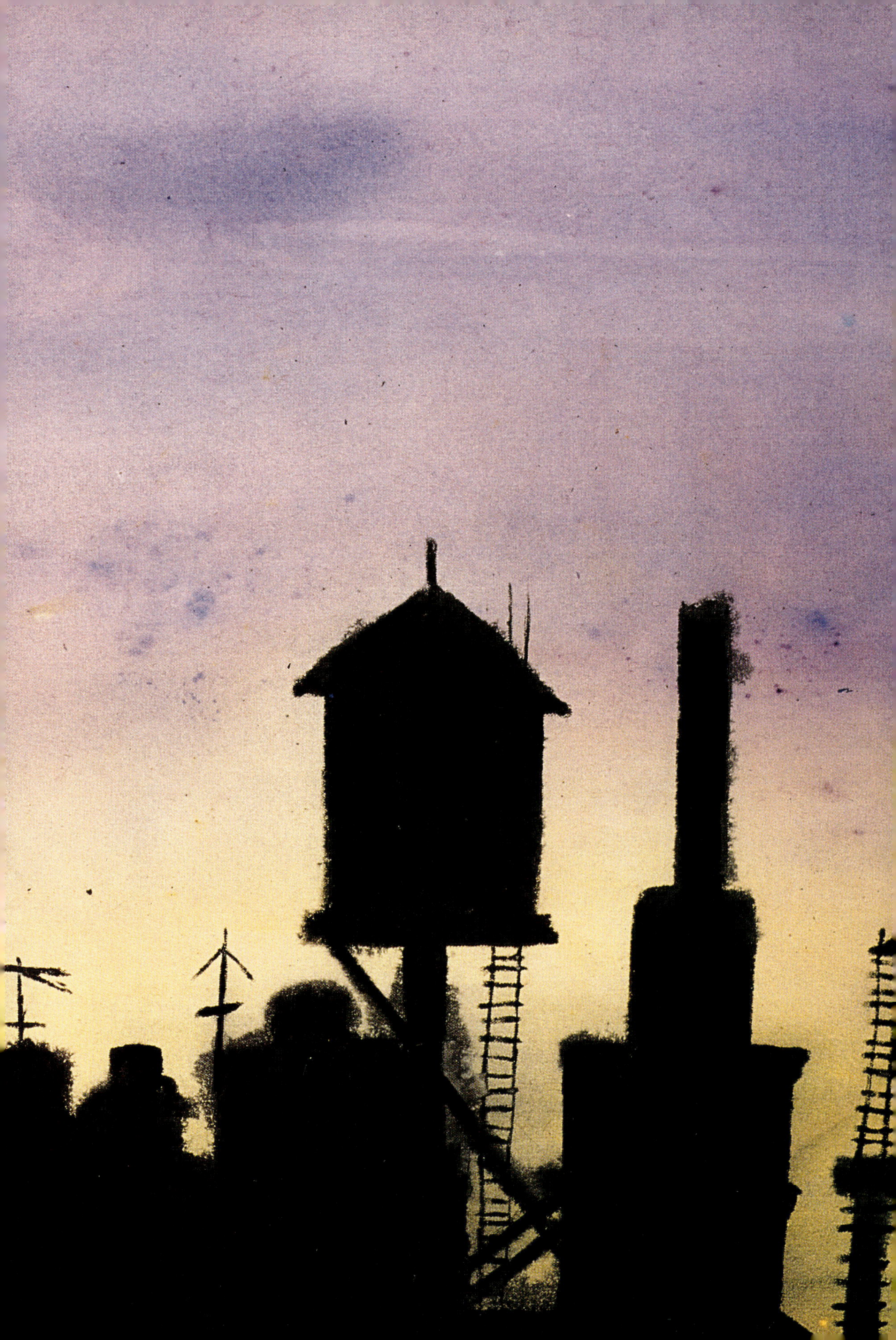

the oldest revolving door,
the park, lighted tops
of ancient towers, where we'd
walked one million times and
taken photographs, past
the building never built,
the lobby never seen,
sheets of energy enveloped us,
182 Fifth Avenue—someone
was home!—Lotus Eaters,
and an image in window Rudy
stopped on, then we all stopped,
mesmerized by twisting lines.
We had a drink with
the paintings, then everything
drifted into a Morganic realm,
where it still is, under
gentle bursts of applause,
a soprano's wicked shout,
baritone's stern rebuttal,
coffee, and another day
of shifting beat positions,
but covered in a distant,
distinct, gauzy well of
having been called again.

*

**the 40th**

The one I really love is not the Jupiter,
it's the 40th. In the first movement, you
are so shaken—it's like math,
perfect and unarguable. An absolute reality
that doesn't exist without people.
There are no trumpets or timpani, but the snow
is plainly visible, and the smell of lotion.
The second movement strings in 3 so deep
you fall in: to be at home drinking wine
listening to Mozart is all, but you
need the wine, because Mozart above all
does not simply exist—he is about tasting
tastes, touching the things one has wanted
to touch, not afraid of fantasies,
knowing, as he wrote to his father, "Death,
properly understood, is the real ultimate object
of our life." The third movement extensions
lurch dissonantly, and the fourth begins
with a hushed abandon that cannot refrain
from shattering nerves and ceilings it hits.
It was the summer of '88,
and the themes were rampant.
A scant three years, and Mozart put
pen to his last page of staves (their
mathematical framework apparent in
reproduction, as his familiar framework)
and sang out his last timpani.
You go down a long, brightly lit
hall, push a door into a room. Someone
takes you by the hand, pulls you
through the crowd and close to her. You
want to clasp something, but the
something has always been just inside you.

*

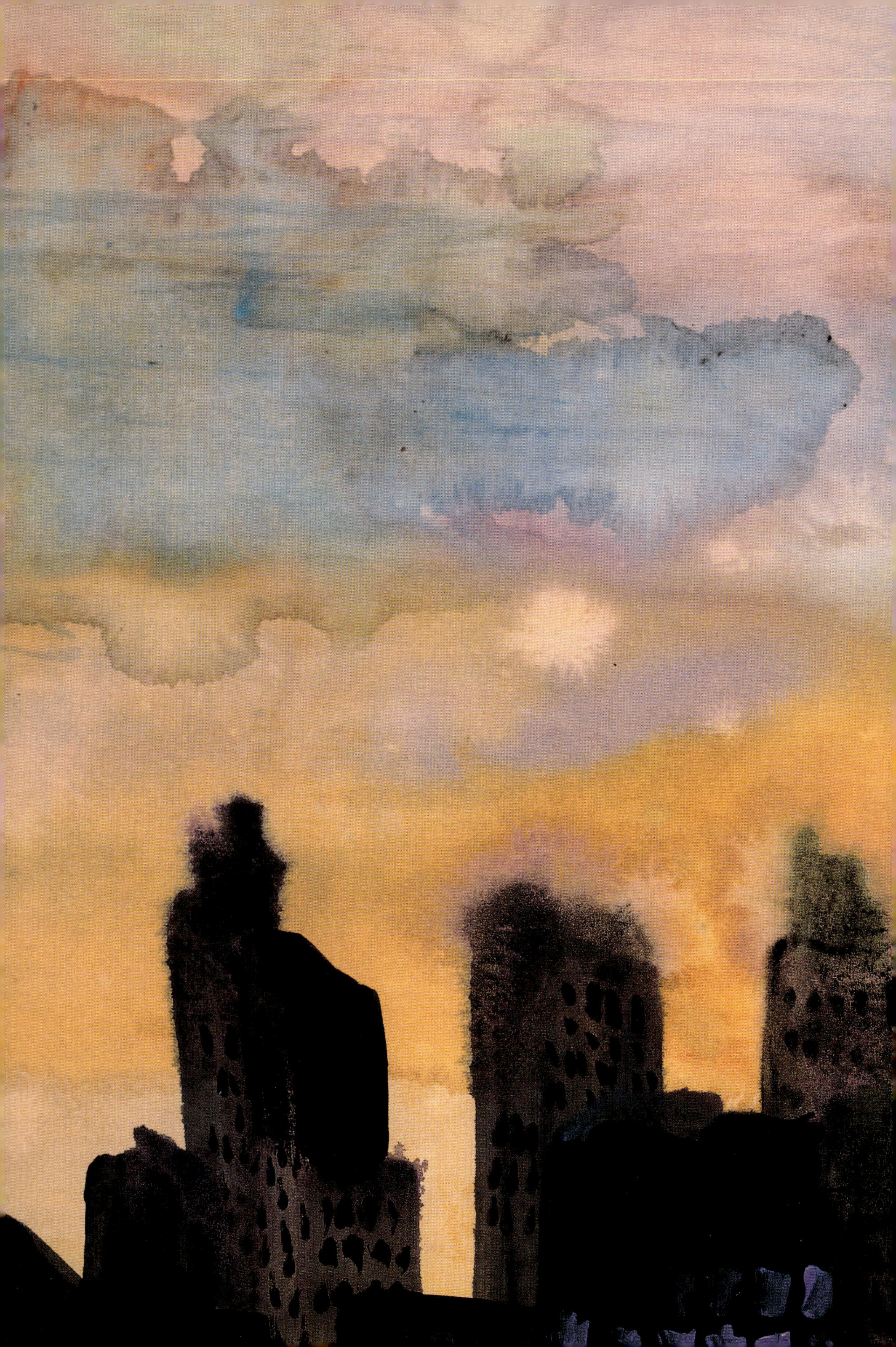

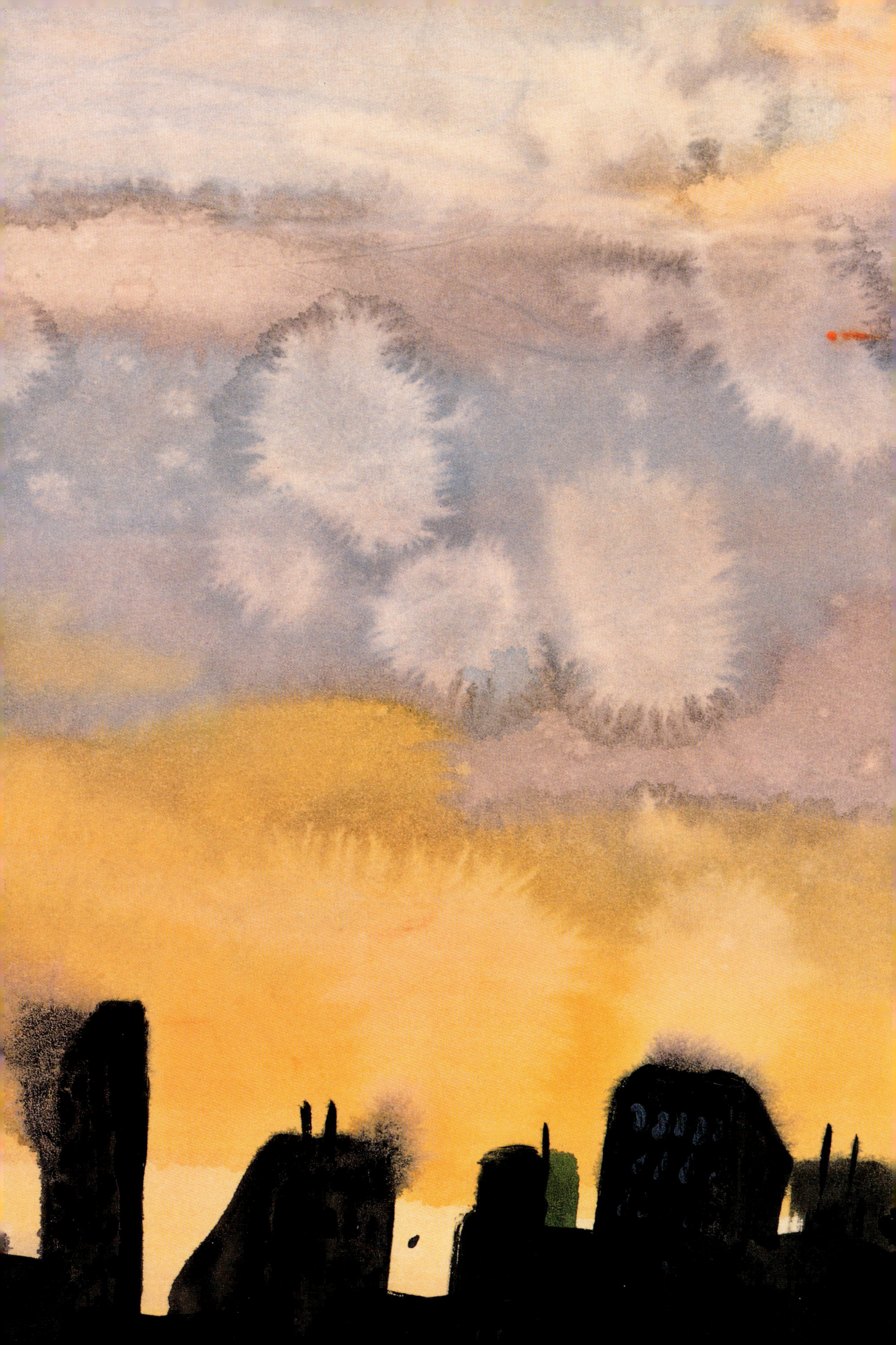

Like the man in the subway jazzing
"As Time Goes By," really playing a bass line
on an old washtub. He smiled and waved,
his coins in a tiny wooden box as
the train pulled out, he kept waving to no
one, his eyes looked up but didn't focus.

*

**Christmas Day**

I was walking and feeling nothing
the sky a gentle color
a jet streak hovered, limpid
suddenly, it was silent
and a feeling of another country,
another life, overtook mine
I was not I, walking in the cold
Christmas was so quiet
a stain on the magazine cover
told one had been there
and alone a meaning convened
where words make a way
we know that streets only
connect us, but what matters
is how the sky looks, how
buildings reflect it, the certain
smell of an air, a day, and
there's never enough,
you go walking through it

*

now I remember he
yeah come on babe
never so shy
that would again be
subjecting it to
the inferior half
maybe it's washed up
maybe I got it wigged
we still got another couple
experiments to make

*

Hi, Nikos!
You let those German sharks come to you!
And remember, Nikos, your face is your sword!
I love you, Nikos. Bye.

—Anthony Quinn as Onassis

*

They don't have much experience dancing.
And each dances only out of what she knows.
Is it bad luck or annoyance mender?
One falls through many spaces, forced
by the heavens' steel to abjure in that painted rapture
you don't know her, cunning will, and to the last
powerful and running over lovers' bounds.
Enough to be remarked as villainous, curling
that body near one like a net, a lure that
streams through air like come

*

A man that courted failure:
and achieved it.

I get real distorted by all of this,
but it's a just distortion.

Yeah, it's all because of ego,
but what's wrong with that?
Are you ashamed of your ego?

Just get a cock and label it.
(Pens are cocks).

*

If Fortuna should smile, perhaps I'd
run away, all unknown and abashed
in a crying, frilly spirit that sustained
me and allowed me to see my life
evolving as something human on this earth
not to be shielded from sun and capable
of visiting the closest spaces,
where a hand always fingers some
empty material, or stoned children
balk at slopping dinner beneath parents'
comatose veins. Eyes start to rust,
then you can't picture yourself
anymore or anyone, except maybe

Let us cease. Long the hour passed
when my head shall be laid to rest.

*

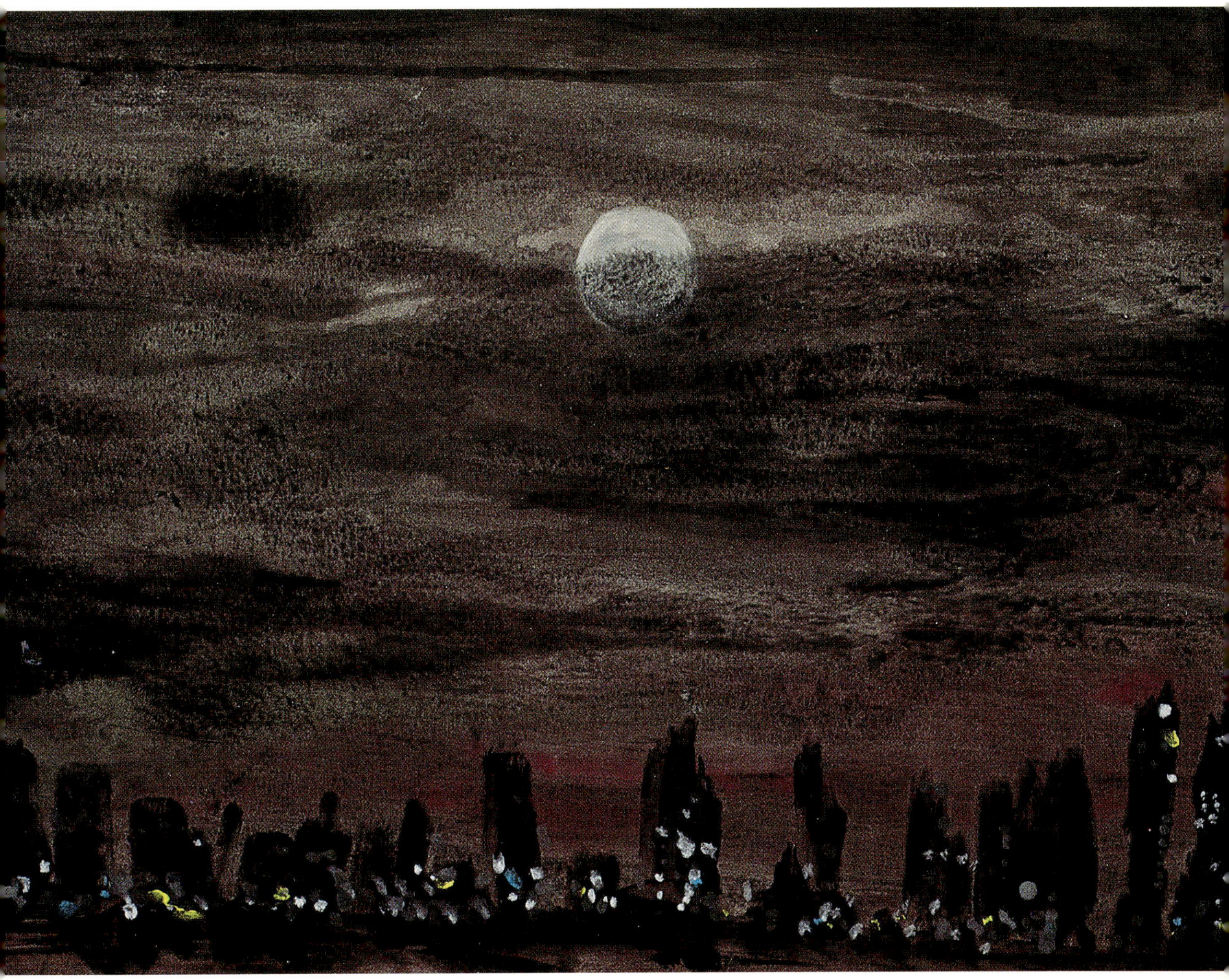

## Pimpin', Maxin'

I'm so lonely and twisted
I just watch these things
on tv, like this movie
with Diana Ross and Billy
Dee Williams—I keep
thinking I should be
like that, but then they're
not even like that, or
maybe I should be like
Liza Minnelli in Cabaret
'what are you hoping for?'
everything is so...plain

the harder I try, the
farther away my dream
seems, so I'm a caricature
actually, this film is great
Tony Perkins is a fashion
magnate, Diana's trying
to break in, Billy Dee's
workin' for the people
(cut to advert for
Bustin' Loose with Richard
Pryor and Cicely Tyson)
so Diana just flew
from Chicago to Rome
and was named...
Mahogany

If you don't make it
here, you'll end up here
I'm supposed to stick
you in a cab and shoot
you to the Drake

it's hard to decide on
much, so much has
slipped away, people hate
and distrust so much
yet I may feel a
community developing
I hate the love lines

*

to think on it were venal
yet, 'twere sin to avoid that venality
it was becoming, it seemed to me,
a situation permitting only one outcome:
should his fist be on your face?
You are unknown dog, whom other
dogs bite glaring in dark, you fall

they are girls with a father who loves them
My pen is my sword, I lash out
at iniquity.  It's all I can.

*

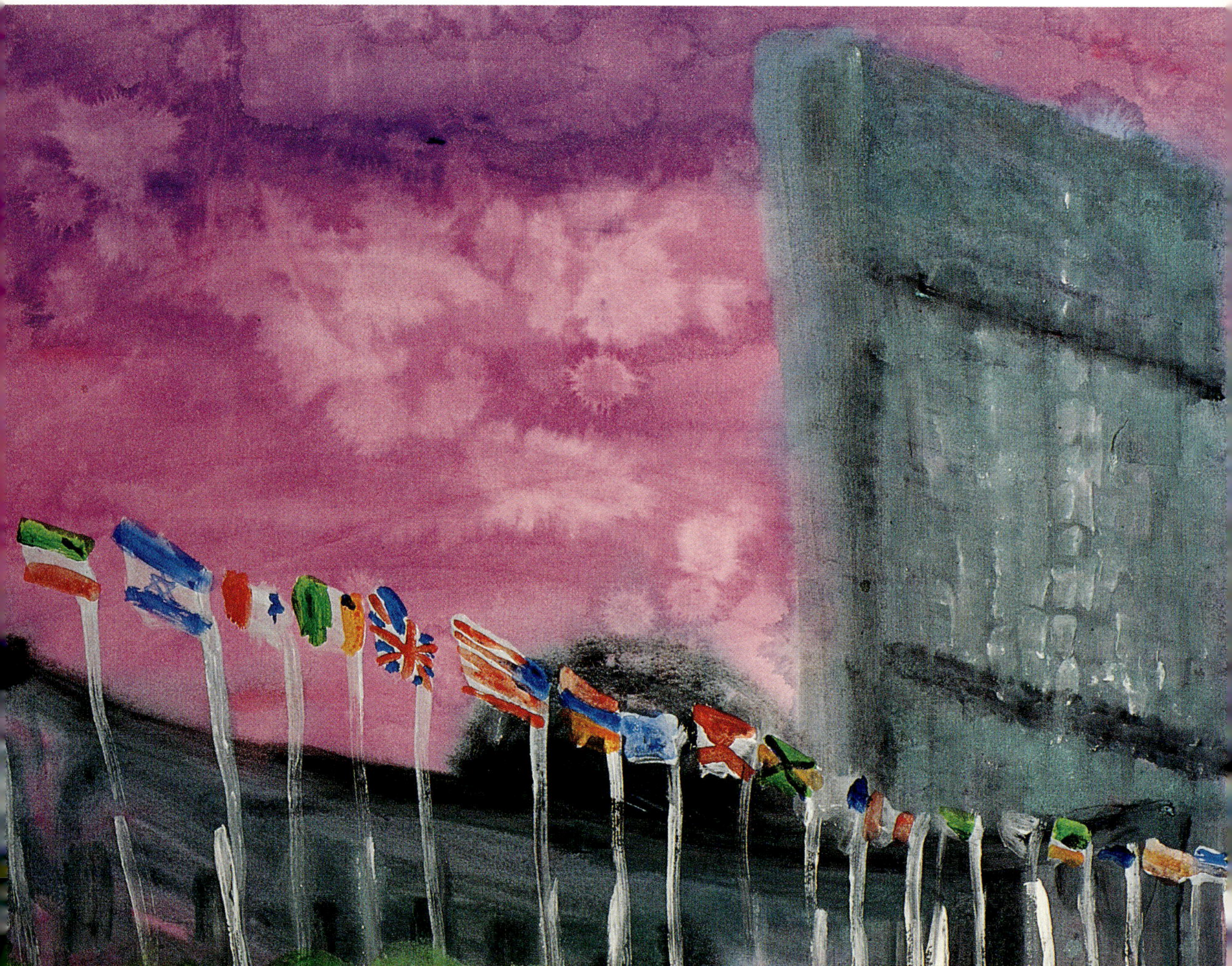

*Anthems From Kings* goes between
The Animals and Aretha.
Cage is right before Cajun.
And John Cale just after.
Greater Than One is between
Stephane Grappelli and Al Green.
Tragic Mulatto between Traffic
and Lennie Tristano,
and Wreck between Hank
Williams and Tammy Wynette.
Meat Beat Manifesto lies between
Paul McMahon and Miles.

My attention had drifted to a table
small and low, littered with complaint,
slow to be excluded. I try to avoid
light stroking the windows. To really
be a comedian, you have to fear
Art Linkletter's daylight with talking
pigeons. Charlie Rose handles the hours,
actors tickle their parts in eyes

I wouldn't grab it vilely
There was a starting up
    from grace,
a sort of abashed willingness
    to listen
in the eyes

*

I hate a poetry afraid to fuck up.
I like a poetry earthbound, flashy,
        sure.
The first rule about drumming:
        Respect the rhythm.
Only great drummers make
        a rhythm alone.
The rest join in.
I have poems I started six years
        ago, or thought about starting,
        that I intend to finish.
That would never happen with a song.
Poetry's fashion moves slower than
songs', and is less relevant.

*

**teorema**

a hand is modeled out toward day
getting stuck in overnight traffic
a hard ring shoots from his nose
and the victims huddle out toward
buildings. In a vial of sunlight,
a little blurt of a day.
because it is considered beautiful
she prepares the congeries.

## Edipo Re

I like to judge people,
and I use my own standard.
This is not wrong,
for the best we can do to
a person is judge them.
A single joke,
and one was prepared
to down them, devastate
the Colonus.
The trips decay down
to ego's remain.

## Medea

it seemed ridiculous
it seemed moving away
from dubbed metal
how far a fixed-rate
loan? another grief
exhibits we won't begin
her delicate displays
and gushing robes
body pushes out to
magic, he understands
woman is strong
man weak

*

$82.5 million shucked from a tree,
and a nonevolved desire to emerge
brings hard pollen to your eyes
and nose, tall grasses shoot up
on periphery of roads, fields—
shots are for about everybody,
attractive colors that turned normal
when someone's symptoms fucked
the size of pills. And you had
never timed to the sounds.
How can they justify themselves?

*

Satch is ready for brain transplant, then requests deferral to Wednesday. "This is Wednesday!" "Wednesday, 1982." Louie is unctuous.

*

a maddening deafness comes over my feet,
a racing head inside my sleeping,
favorites of stage and screen; a bygone age.

*

When you are a miniature,
your glands give reason,
windows you passed nine
years, even you have
manufactured face,
a torrent resigns of
fecund wraith

another way to pin
head to size is fervent
in springing upward
a sign is protected
as among sleepers
you are forwarded

*

**Memorial Day**

it's nice to have a day to do absolutely nothing in,
especially if that day is the nicest day
of the year, and Memorial Day, or even
better, the day before the Day itself.
For on the Day is this triumphant surge
of youth and energy pumped into the drain
of it ending—I am always flushed at the end
of Memorial Day. It is the day I intersect
with those nodes or interstices of past days.
But today has the languor of knowing it all to come.
I should be outside. But in here is so perfect—
light blowing through window shades. It will never end.

It is six thirty and feels like morning.
What's to be admired in Charlie Parker is not
his dexterity, it's his mind. Like that other
temperamental genius who died young, he knows just
where to put the notes, but, like Kerouac
says, every phrase Parker plays has wit—
hello to Red or you, or he'll drop out mid-phrase
and leave the piano player comping. Waking up,
he throws in some flourish just before the Horn

comes crashing in again. But it's the shape
of his mind that stays in one's memory, the fullness
of his tone, the way his races scare you.

Then suddenly the day is over. It is only now
an image, faintly scudding in a thought-swept
sky, of how and why it could have been something.

*

**30**

I am suddenly happy to become 30.
It has a big sound to it.
What have I done to justify being 30?
Today is my birthday.
Yesterday, I had a wild party.
There were fortunes and bread.
This guy kept telling me
my beads were Mexican,
Allen quizzed him which
city in Mexico. We
listened to Charlie Parker,
Rebel MC, and Athena arrived.
We were all pleased, as
I'd only invited her that day.
Francesco and Alba left with
Elizabeth, their dog. We
saw *Open Letter* and performed
"Your The DJ," drank
a lot and danced sambas. Wander
whirled a white sheet about
his head! I like birthdays.
Because you really get to see

what you are like. I like
getting presents. I respect
them to the extent
I believe they were given.
And I regard the presents I give
exactly the same. Frank Lima's
a class act—a bottle of Veuve.
The shape and size and smell
of the painting Hunt gives me
all thrill me, even before looking
at the painted image. Allen
gives me *Songs of Innocence and*
*Experience*. When he arrived,
about 12, he floated over to
where I was dancing with Babs
to P-Funk. He was wearing a
very light white jacket over
a blue shirt and white pants.
He seemed very light. Today
I pushed Alice in the swings
for a while. She is such a
perfect girl. Now the day
has dawned again on me—
for the 10,950th time. That
doesn't seem like an awful
lot of days, when you add
them up, one by one. As I feared,
everything looks the same, except
my eye, which has come to
the understanding that some days
are sacred. And to hold anything
less than that is to be
simply playing a part.

*

"Dancing Days"

"Stand"

"Family Affair"

"Earth Blues"

*

my favorite moment in Miles
is the beginning of "Sivad,"
cuica rampant on the
upbeat—everything
crystallizes about Miles.
Unlike Hendrix' wildness,
every beat is systematically
regimented into a huge skeleton.
segue into "Love Divine," off
*Love, Devotion and Surrender.*

*

"Lila's Dance"

*

## FUMBLE

If you see the guy asleep on the train,
and the K-Mart out in the distance,
and you hear Harry Belafonte sing "Brown Skin Girl,"
you know you just have to try harder
Your nations are coming, your Specials
followers (and Selecter) you can do
anything you want—ska was such
a great English invention, like House
you greet it in your doorway, it grabs
your coat, puts hat on your head, and
you're out for your next beer
or Bob Marley intoning

> I want to disturb my neighbor
> 'cause I'm feelin' so right
> I want to turn up my disco
> blow them to full watts tonight
> in a rub-a-dub style
> in a rub-a-dub style...

Have you ever thought about what
it means to live "in a rub-a-dub style"?
"Soon we'll find out who is the real revolutionaries"
You have to make your own rules
you have to give it more, like a flower you
saw blooming today on a vine
Digital Underground are
as grand as Miles and Dizzy
and so essential that it's verbal

Bootsy is precise as Bird
we're travelling through Connecticut,
old factories lit up in night
A man in a furry Kangol cap
waits for the head, George Clinton
gets a call from Prince, it's all
out there, that funked-out keyboard
(Dance, sucker!) What have you
thought about, do you see
things any way that is something, yet?
Now there is only true
funk to be sought, a way of communing
with your time, a time when
you were alive is revived
all the rainy nights alone in Chicago
signify something, can look
the window in the face

*

**Vanitas**

I'm 30, my cock and ass are perfect
put your fingers beneath my balls
I walk on Canal Street's western pediment
mesmerized by the highway lights
I've poured my love so many years into her concrete
Looking down, I see the De Kooning paintings
I love them

*

He doesn't have the vaguest idea
what music is, nor does he—
it's a statement about yourself
in the weekend, it all gets crowded
with losers from Jersey
a vast boom decorates my leg
and I realize I have acted out
a pageant, fooling even myself

*

## TO A ZONE

I never did anything wrong
my friend is in Paris
rain works in circles
on our feet, October, cringing
that it is not cold yet
the signs on the street are scary,
all about killing your friend
and Hitler, men piss against
sides of buildings, a new culture
is grouping in Japan, and you get
these voices on your speakers,
nearby, strange, I take things
from the past and use them—
wear them (the pink pants,
the plaid windbreaker Billy gave me)
or think about what they said
but I don't look for continuity
everything's so always old
I would kill myself, I try to resist

The Charlatans, but they're
playing in my head, you take in
streetlights, powdery days,
my head reminds you of them
I've got a strong zone

*

I hear them laugh at me
I turn and see their faces
My tall hat and long beard
  are ridiculous
But I know their pain
for I look into the eyes
of every one of them

*

**MARIA CALLAS January 1991**

Paris...1958

Her voice is so good you feel unease in its presence
Its masculine tension quavers innocently
The drummer is massive. His cock
Is massive as Amalfi.

Opera, more than any other "classical" music,
Builds to climaxes, whose ecstatic bursts
Of energy resemble the gospel service
More than anything else. Everyone in Paris
Coming at the same time.

*

I'd listen but there was only the sound,
no sex to be spoken of. Around
the corridor, a private illumination
had taken place, her hand
melted with the hardness
of the future

*

## ELEGANS

What is vaster, the impediment of night sky
or one's own terrible longing?

I had to abandon that security
to know another security.

You'll be forever tripping down
that staircase.

You must be elegant,
but elegant *means* contemporary.

*

Those tiny sybaritic touches
around toes or knuckles are
enough to send him skimming,
shining through an opening
too aloof to allow him. He looked
anyway, but two faces always
prevented him. Anyway, her odor

succumbed to daily expenses, as
women move nearer the secular
flame of manhood. Their marching
crunching cries are redemptive
and recall our men falling
at Grenoble. A noble event,
but one failing to elicit sympathy,
forever tied to lingering fear,
cadences that erupted, summer
inside a tear—her embraces
warned him a simpler time
was coming and one less able
to receive the energies
of a failing system.

*

**A Pool and A Dream**

plunged ahead of us

a whole sound eluded his eyes
when no poodle of disrespect
could foresee. Tangelos arose
from a need to cause, frozen
to your head, unwinningly
prized from oneself, again
overlooking the deceit, one
dreadful skin in the oars of
one movie. Other men

searched for items that told
him fathoms from shore
a boat was tugging him,
her hands adrift in the
confidences of morning.

*

What's Quincy Jones thinking?
It's a little hypothetical,
but probably, "Oh boy, I
could get good danish here!"
Each new one brought
insects he could see
and one
even wrote that everything
had emptied off his head.
Night breezes ripped his hand
from the hood—"Why do you
call out?" he cried, protecting
her in a grin that drove
back yesterday's grimace.
Have you howled at a roast?
Dried out over figs?
Nothing's as it was, but
that is proper. And so
is that heavy weight
crushing your neck.
Goodbye.

*

## NOT YOU

I pick up Eileen's book and listen
to cracks in the ceiling. Every
now and then it takes two to
tangle the thread of awareness,
or is it just being of the city? One
way we are evicted is alive, through
a great mound of expressed desire.
When she speaks, a great moan
emanates from within, and they wait
in line for her. Ever notice the
blue lining in a peach salad? diseased
hair like rent is living, perturbed
into essence, the like ol' Harvey woulda
scoffed at. In essence, it is a
freak show, and the freaks are smarter
than their "owners." We let our
freak flag fly. It's like those two
lesbians at the solidarity march two years
ago. They took off their shirts
on bright Hudson to the video camera.
Their breasts were free.

*

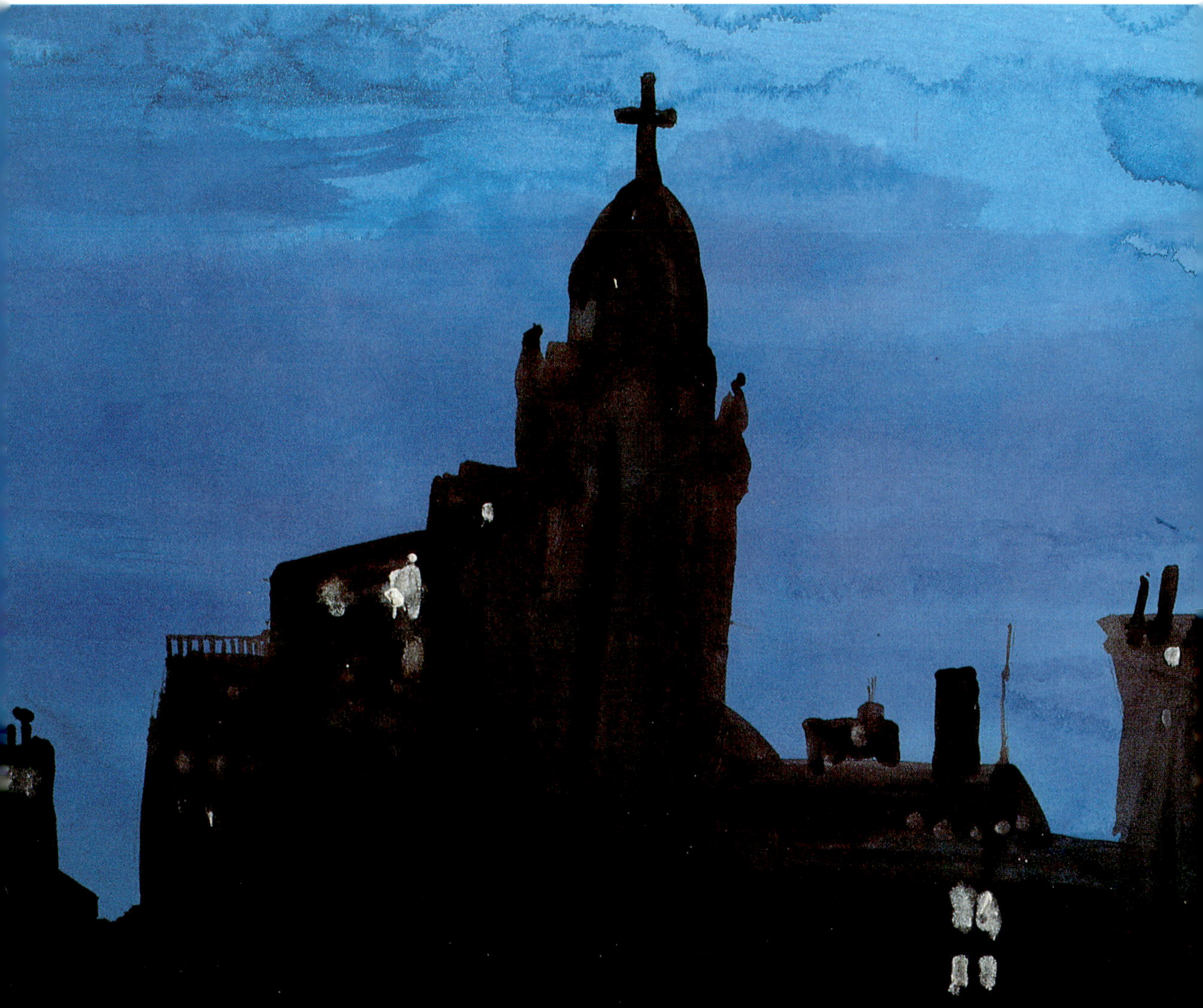

Reality is a daytrip
through the back of your hand,
a poem so complete
it is coherent, brings
cold restaurants, trains,
to mind, why did you
stay—10 years ago—
in that bedroom over-
looking train tracks,
a secret was shared,
something you've got
so beyond, sometimes
it's dizzy as you go
up, and up, and you
never come down, you just
keep spiralling somewhere
not closer to what you were,
but not farther, enough
is inside to insure you
will not again be bolted
from, outside the place
you all made sense,
before twisting into weird
confusion, swift denial
of joy, and madness.

*

Although mordant,
her usual fire
protected us from
looking on her,
for she's composed
of small materials,

so finely conjuged
to make fitting
a century's game.

*

The doe leaned against a fence,
a reprieve opened us from wanting,
but fences were erected where once
cookies had been exchanged, a bartered
boy locks his belongings in a trunk.
Copulating teenagers

he emptied out whole sounds
of lateness, a summer hung over
them as Jack Lemmon is forced
to go sun,
you should be able to track
your errors, or at least
find ways of excluding them
from reunions and breakfast.
Why don't you try?
You've got a lot of brightness
right behind your eye.
(eyelid is vast pull
of Planet of the Apes)

You get captured, then you escape:
That's kind of how it works.
You keep a daily intensity.
Their jokes are humorous but suave.
No more meetings!
It's Monday night.

*

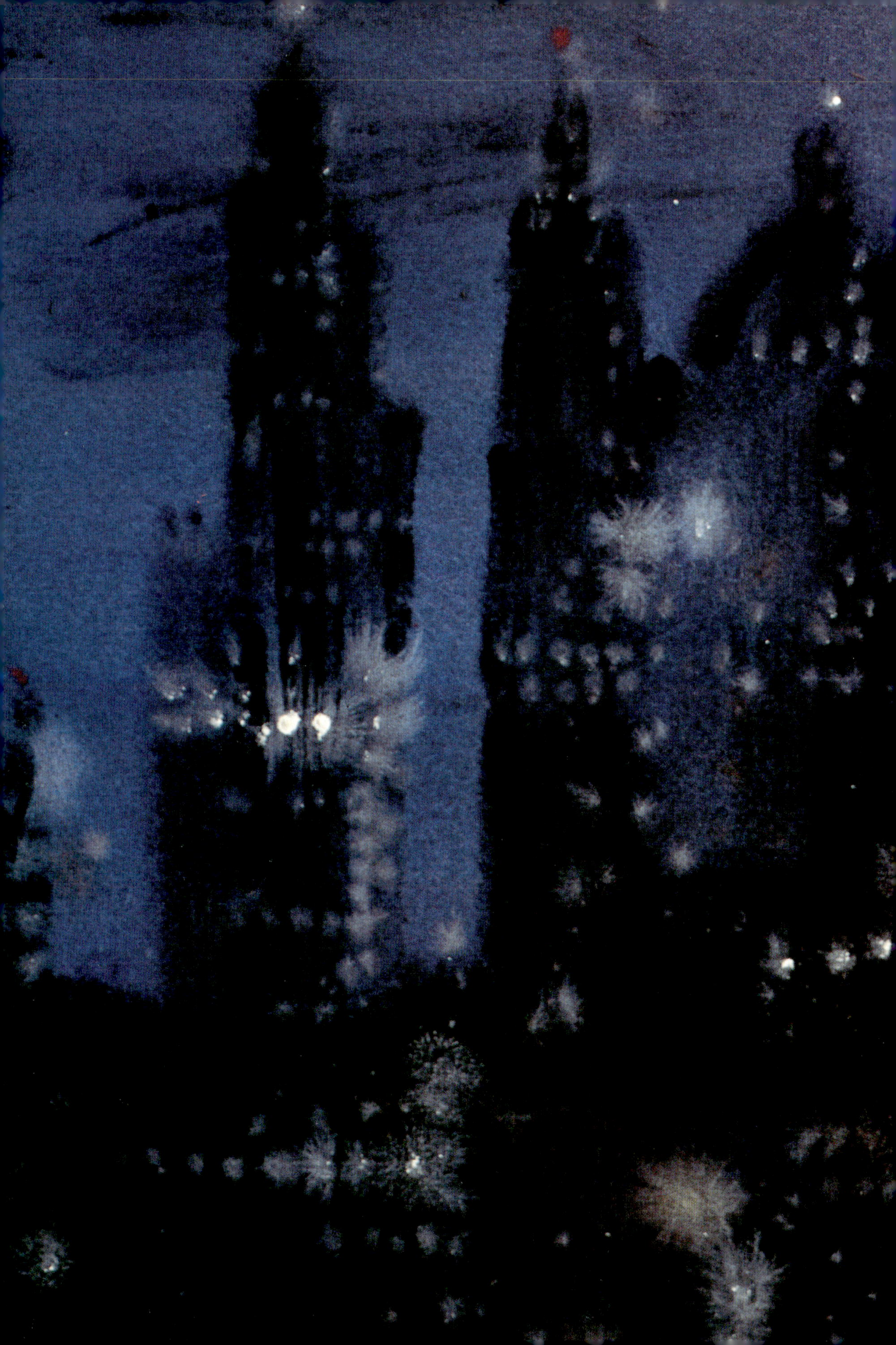

I have a friend who lives in this place.
I can't write "poems" any more.
Don't think about it much.
Just drive to the place it gets you to.
Try to find a body that fits yours.
Did you ever elapse on a subway?
I did it was painful. I'm not
avoiding punctuation, just denying
it the power to change my life.
My life goes its trajectory.
I've forgotten people I used to hate.
Usually I just fall off a deep edge,
I hear a scream growing near a rock,
a violent cloud strains to be heard,
someone is breaking up in my sleep.

*

*Farewell To The Planet Of The Apes*
Roddy McDowall is a cute ape
hockey is fascinating, Jimmy's
in the hospital

*

My favorite summer (1956), I
won the triple crown—.353, 52 homers,
130 rbi's. What many don't know
is I also began a secret affair with the trainer,
a tall, muscular man.
On days off, we'd drive out
to distant locations, drink beer,
and make passionate love.
Then I'd come back and be
The American Hero. As the season
drew to a close, and Ted Williams
hotly pursued me for the batting
title, my relationship to Dick
grew strained. I couldn't take
the pressure. So I called a press
conference and told all. It was
a great relief to be known as
the first bisexual triple crown winner.

*

a violet blur on a down leg
flying human in masks
when they call it's the same hard
and simple way to shoot the cells

*

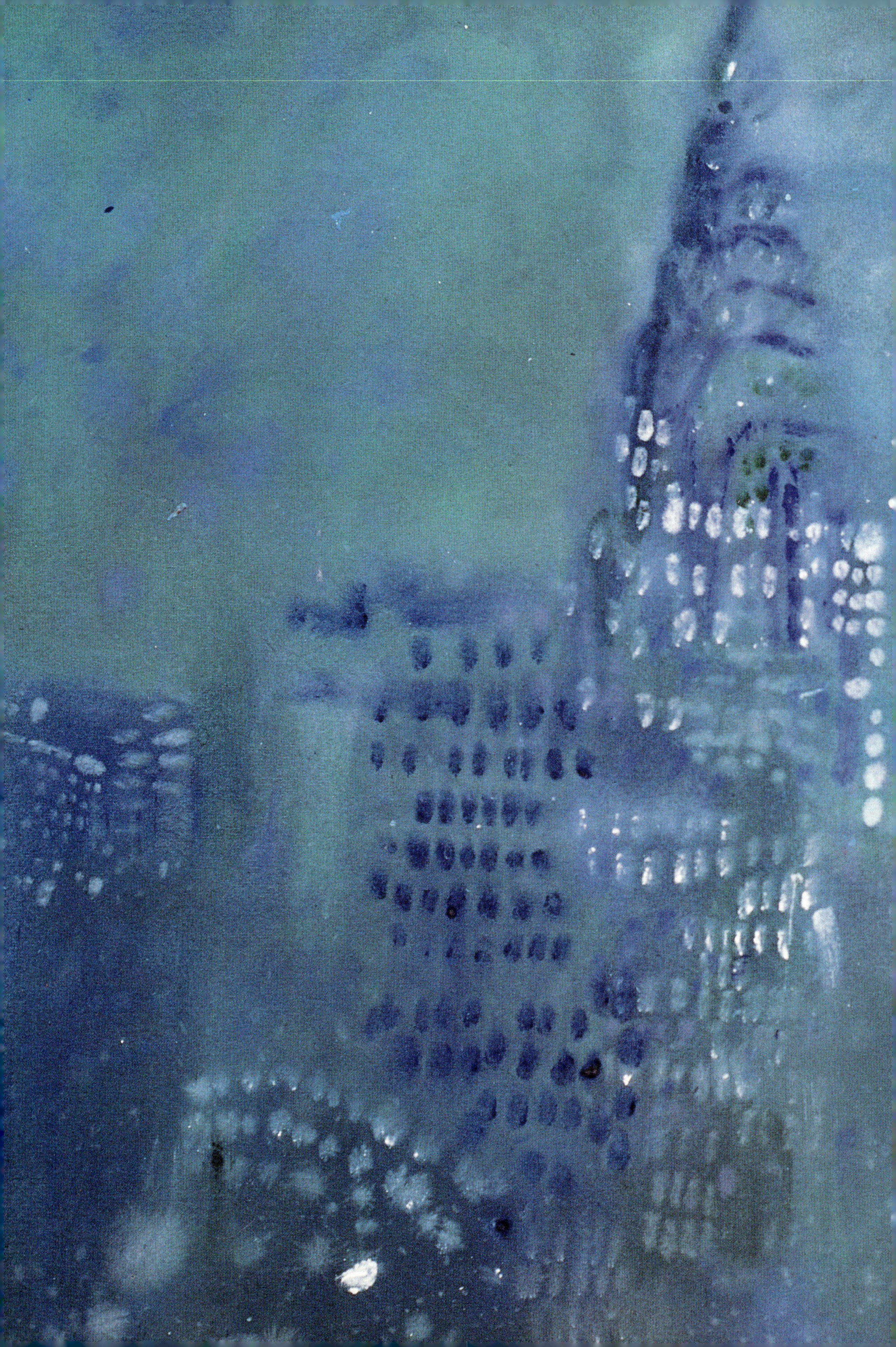

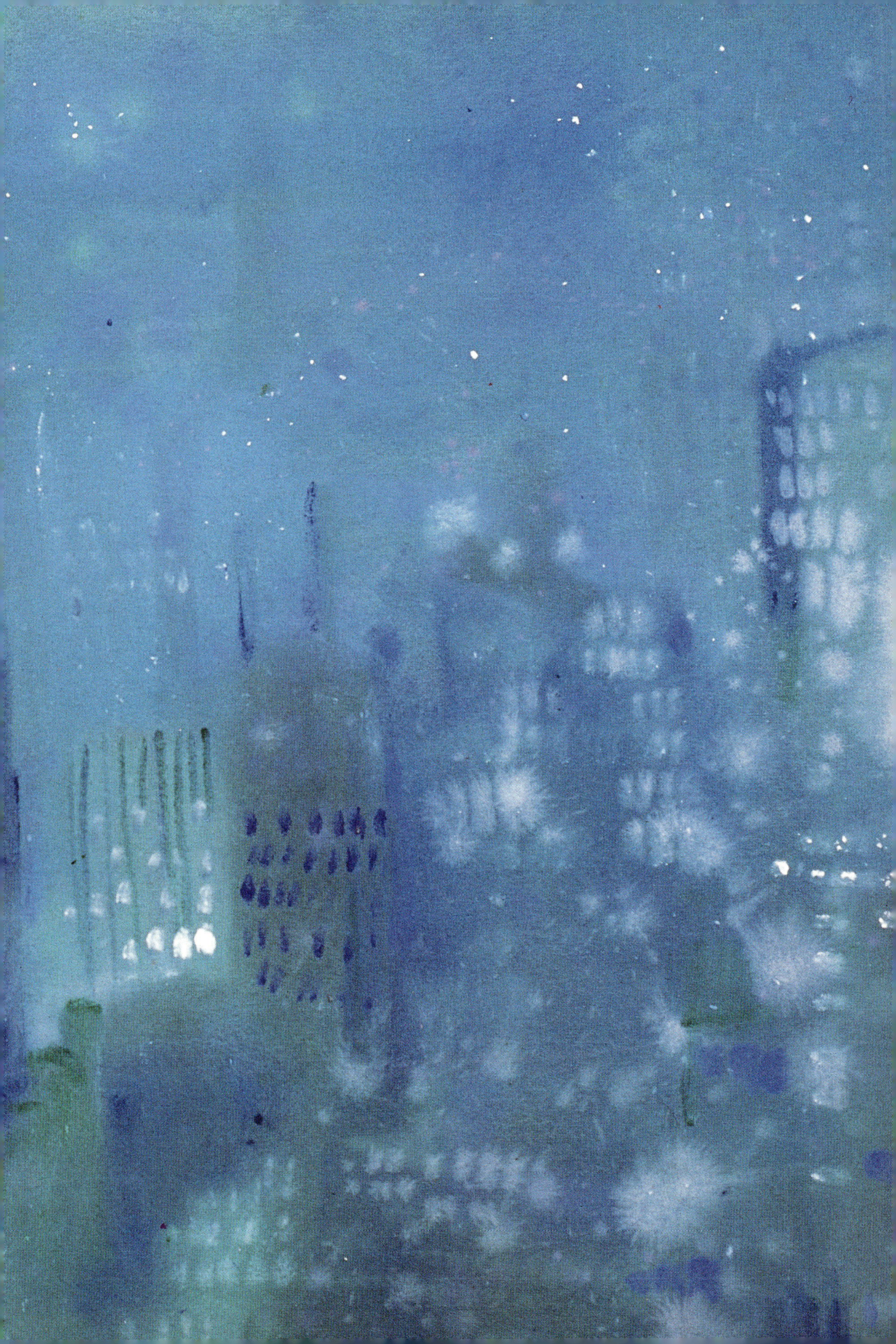

Every time you entered my life,
you destroyed me. Now it's my turn
to destroy something. She's a
sensitive ape. Now we're chillin',
with EPMD. A single excessive
urge is all that dominates them,
but they fall prey to conflicting
impulses, die laughing as spurts of
water jet from their eyes, close
starlings circle the reservoir. Under-
neath, a silent wailing, as of girls,
brings the deejay to crack his record,
the couch potato to stuff his set,
that blank window unto dying.
With so much as repeated advertisement,
he orders them to sing, which is
one of the things they remember
from grammar school. The poet
died, and I caught myself writing poetry.

*

"Never fuss about a room."

I saw him Thursday, and two days
later he is dead. Poetry's biting stream
has flowed through him and ceased. He
caused us to examine our sleeping,
bright epithets arose from his way
of calling. And the timer pings.
He had a way of focusing, of letting
the detail be transported into
something huge and white like
the Vatican. He couldn't speak
on Thursday, but seemed to understand
us. I held his hand. He grabbed
me tight. Trucks took the garbage
away. Two toes were missing.
He indicated he wanted the sheet
off, then dragged it back.
I was going to give him a copy
of my book, then decided to mail it,
since he couldn't hold anything.
He greeted transatlantic boat
travellers, but had no time
to wear them out. A steady,
single hum pervaded his life,
miming Truth & Justice, till
a damp array of verdure tumbled
toward me, allowing me to see him
as I always had: a seer able
to react and a creator bent
to originate. I hallucinate.

*

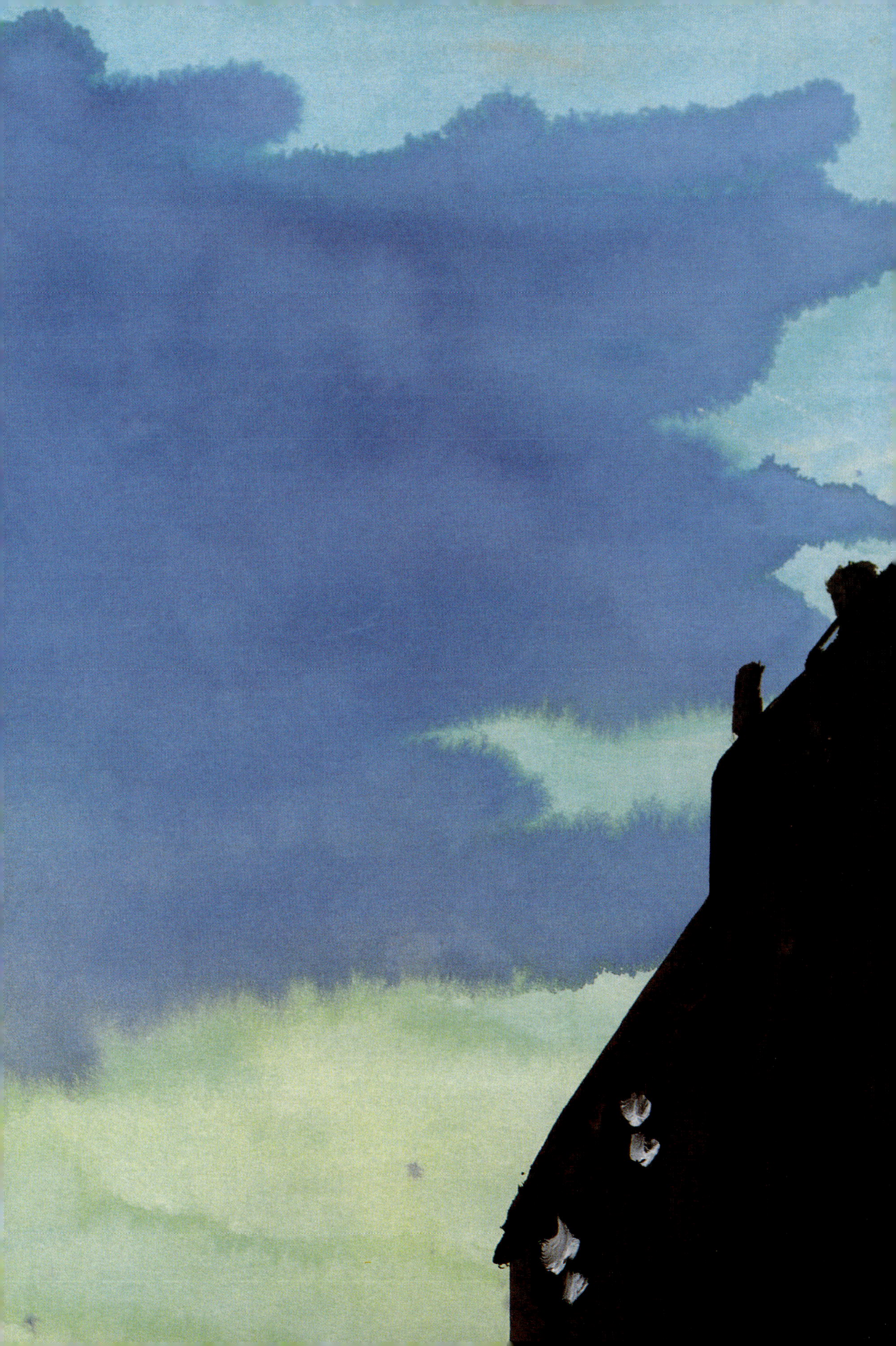

He pressed on past her, his truth
afire and glowing. He pressed her
as she sped to their deaths.

*

## Per Diem

We spent all night on the boat with a light like
sunrise went James Merrill in his poem "Samos"
he recited it and "The Broken Home" earlier
I read a poem by Carlos Drummond de Andrade
I walked up Broadway and bought a pair of white Levis
A strange weight held my calla lily I wondered
what John Ashbery would do tonight
I had two different teas Elliott Sharp
called I'm wearing a linen jacket,
green shirt, new pristine Levis, black,
'60s Euro style suede hightop shoes
"I'm gonna ram this down their throats"
Ilka and Luigi lent me Sarou, this French singer
I had a Cran-Grape Charlie Morrow
gave me Word Merrill ruled the podium
like a lord, finely groomed and with a
magisterial sadness approaching Horace
in sublimity and regal care of conception
I gave him a copy of *New York Hello!*
and saw him warmly kiss a man hello
the piano arrived, a piano is so different
from a keyboard, Vivien played Brazilian
pieces, then we went to Jimmy's funeral
everybody was there, it was exactly
the same huge crowd that heard

him at Dia, now they heard him again, he
vastly left their lives, John was supposed
to introduce Merrill but couldn't, someone
read "Korean Mums" then Merrill was reading,
in the same room Jimmy had given that
first public reading, when I saw him
in St. Vincent's the other day he couldn't
form words but looked good, attentive
and apparently comfortable, someone
calls from Brazil asking about S.F., and
Haight-Ashbury reminds me of John Ashbery,
the immense world Jimmy has given us

*

**Pearl**

Jimmy was always so kind. When I was
a kid, he bought me two Janis Joplin albums,
*I Got Dem Ol' Kozmic Blues Again, Mama* and
*Pearl*, and another time he gave me the
classic Kinks album *Arthur*. On that album,
the Kinks reached a textural height
with songs like "Brainwashed" and "Young
And Innocent Days." Jimmy was right
with it. As he wrote, "Look at your hand—
it's real." He wrote me a letter which
said, "Bruno says to tell Sunny—but
I can't make out the rest." The two dogs
never did meet, and he would send me a
dollar for Christmas. Now, at 2 am, it rains.
The kind of rain Jimmy would have noticed.

*

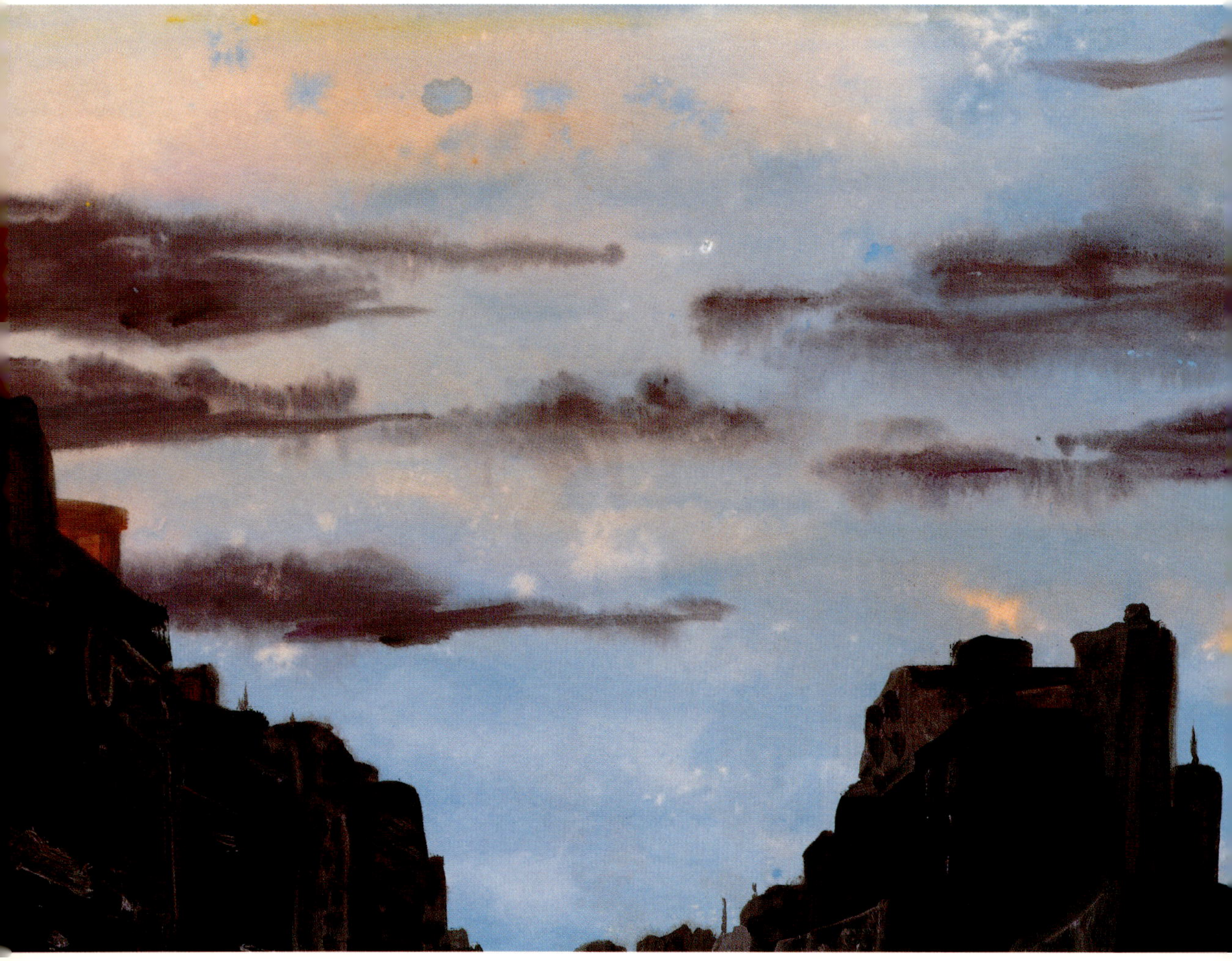

Another blight, another fight.
Everyone's sleeping in polychromy
chambers alight with tower's
roof, and cold soups allow
a cough. With words, we won
a way down a dark thicket,
where you lay holding A Book
Of Dreams, floating lazily
above the crackup, flares
huddled like eyes above them.
Scientists with dark wanders
hovered about the site, about
to unleash a crushing truth
on a frivolous, disrespectful
world. Her breasts hover in
taffeta: there is a word for
that, for when she ceases
to exist…

Poetry is mentioned in passing,
We are aware of the best poem
we have ever read—"To The
Taxes" by Vernon Eubanks.
A master of expressionistic detail,
each whimper from the cover
of her lip is pablum to our
ear, we have come so used
to her plaint. But she is useful
in other ways, and wise. She
among us told us our parents
would be back, to witness the gifts
they planted among us.

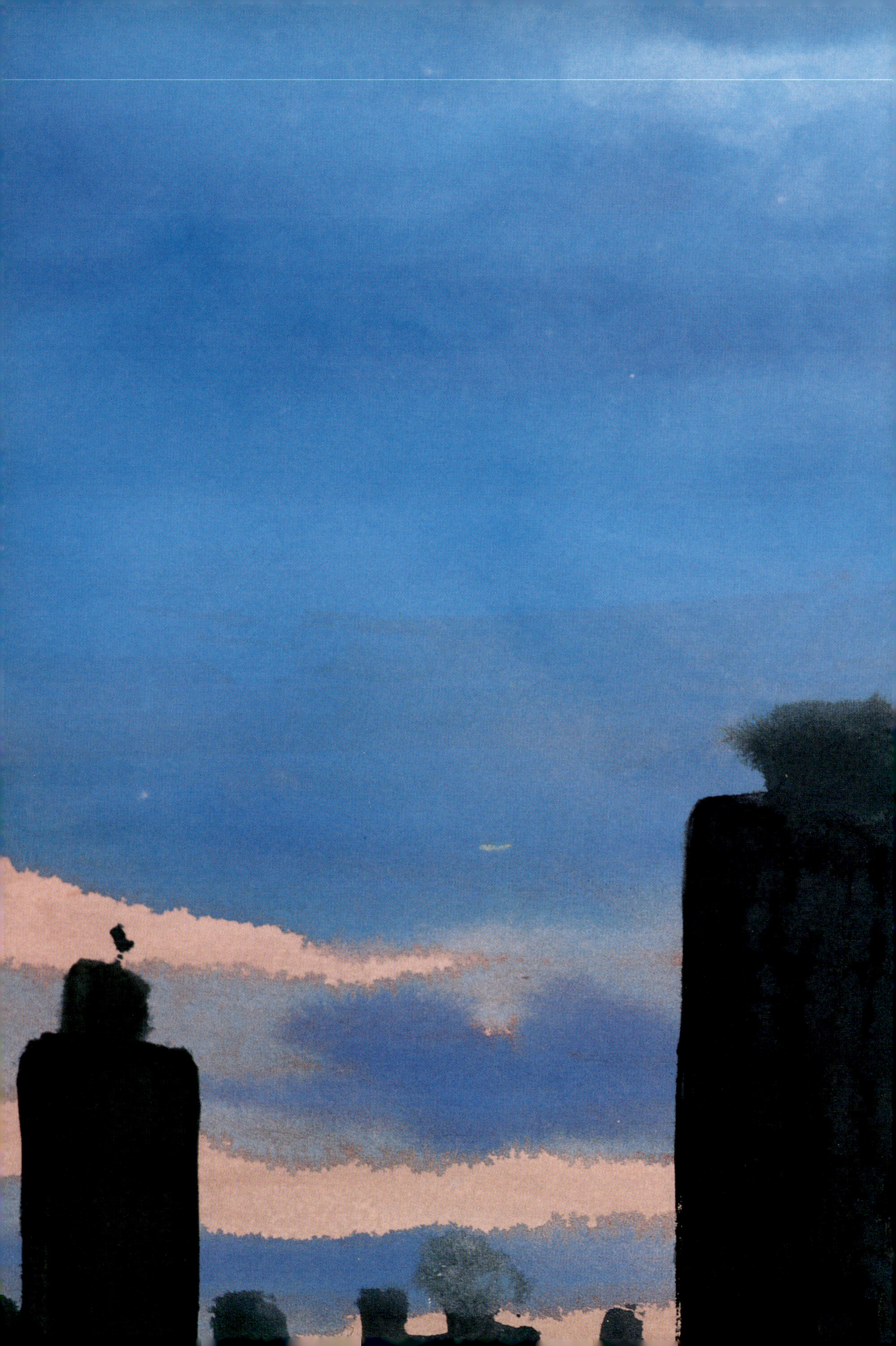

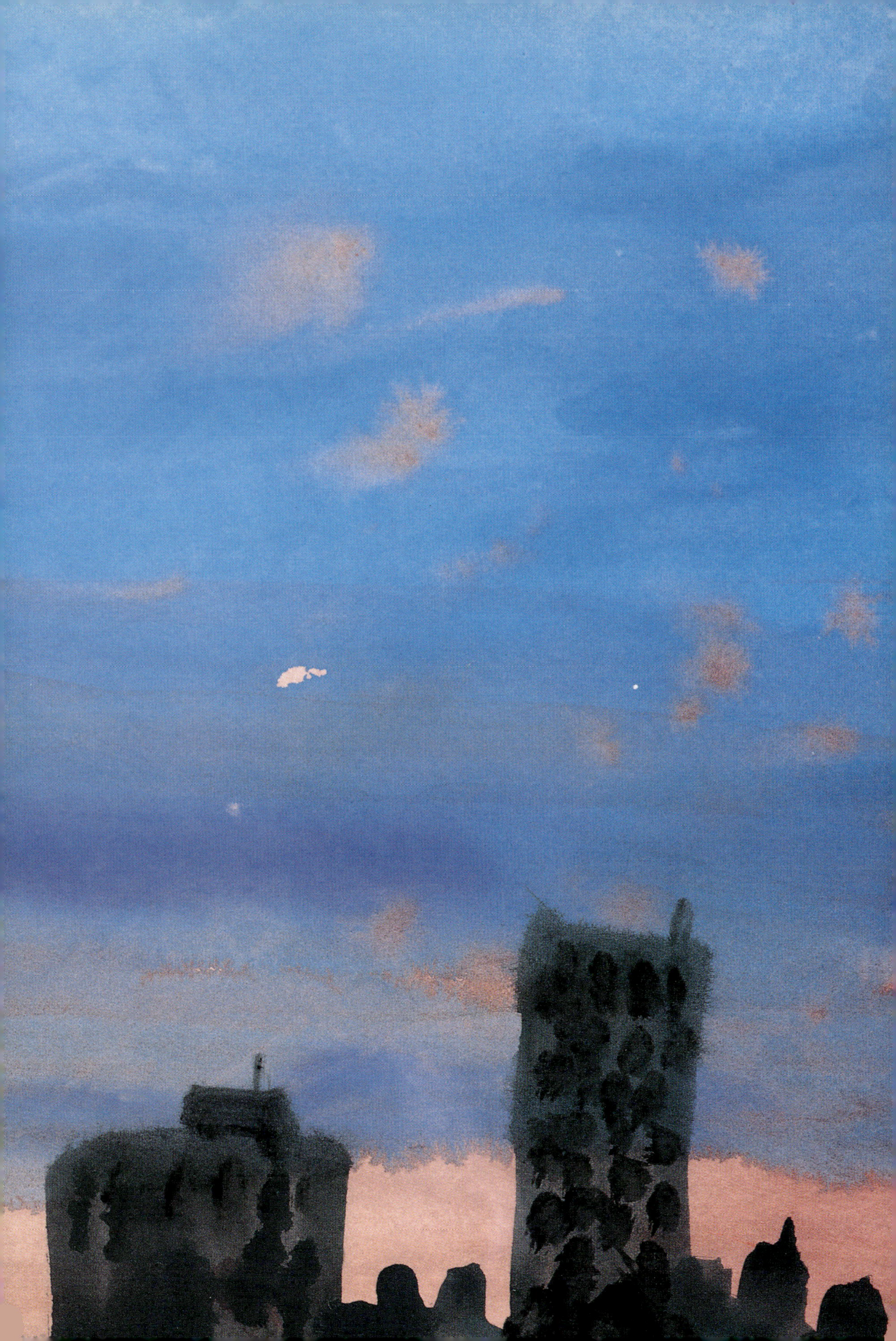

They would be back in the distant
future, observe, and vanish,
this time for good.
But no one seems to know
what type of tree had killed
him or to care.
She was getting dressed,
I was trying to make sense of it.

*

Again, always from the signs
making reason of it even
now it is so dark to see.
You would retire, your
gentle strength would fail you
utterly. Let's begin again.

In General Hospital, the question
always is who's going to operate.

*

At reading two day old
Henry funny, Ash unrelenting
made me like it more
that was a good time
banged out of my senses!
banged out of my senses,
I begged anyone to go.
The tour bus pulled up slowly,
mascara shading her frizzy
hair. I wasn't really

hiding anything.
Big blasts of hair, rising from
They have no idea
who I am. I keep
nodding in a way
that suspects them.
It's usually pretty
loud. Goodbye.

*

Inquest of ears,
sudden dimming.
I am slowly
achieving consciousness.
A finely rolled
joint of two
marijuanas and
hashish. And,
I might add,
of such dimension
that the paper—
"Le Zouave"—
circles only
once, leaving
the dark verdure
apparent. It
smells a little
of bacon, or
washed churches,
Cristiana's tears,
a pimp.

*

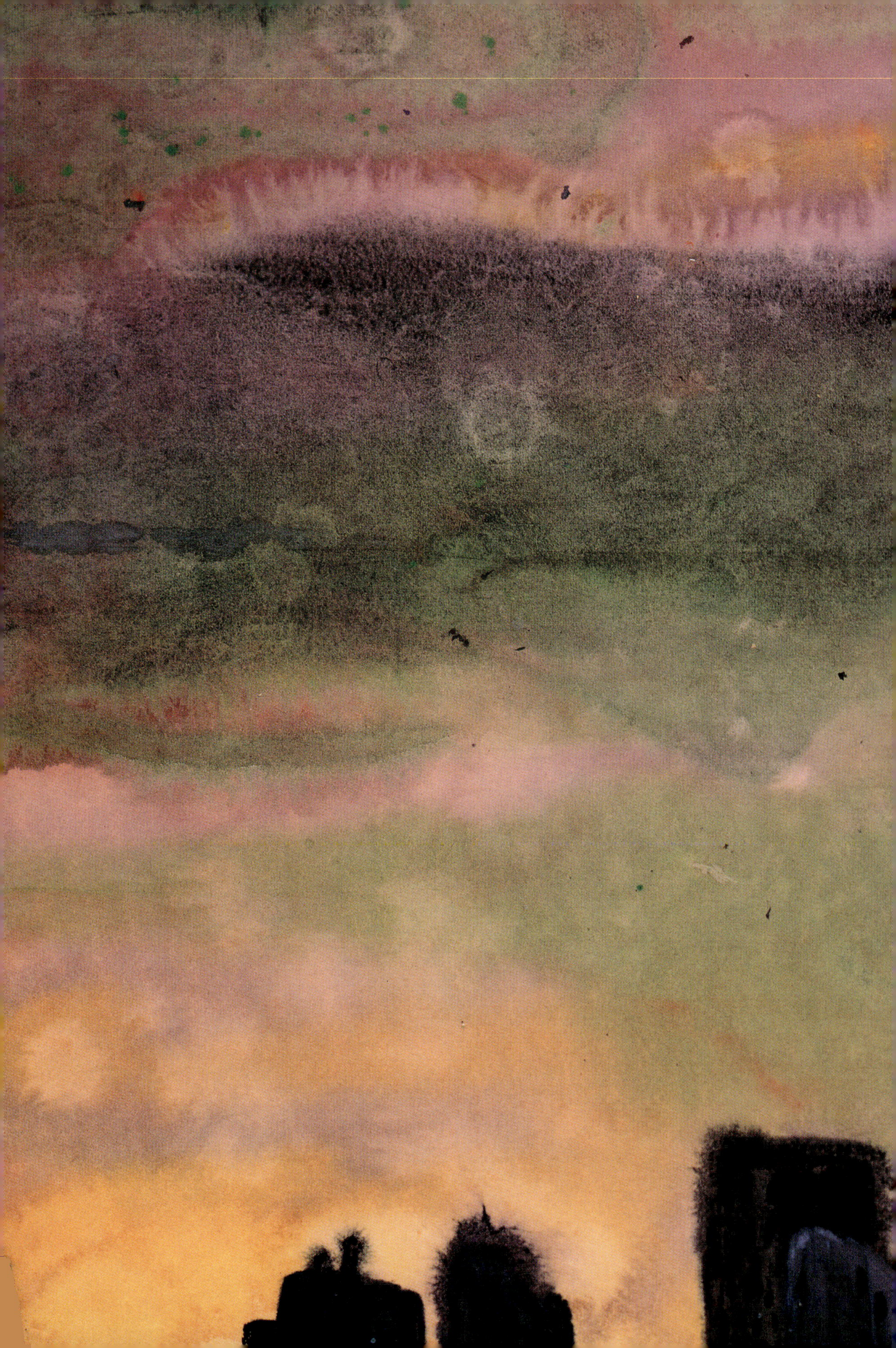

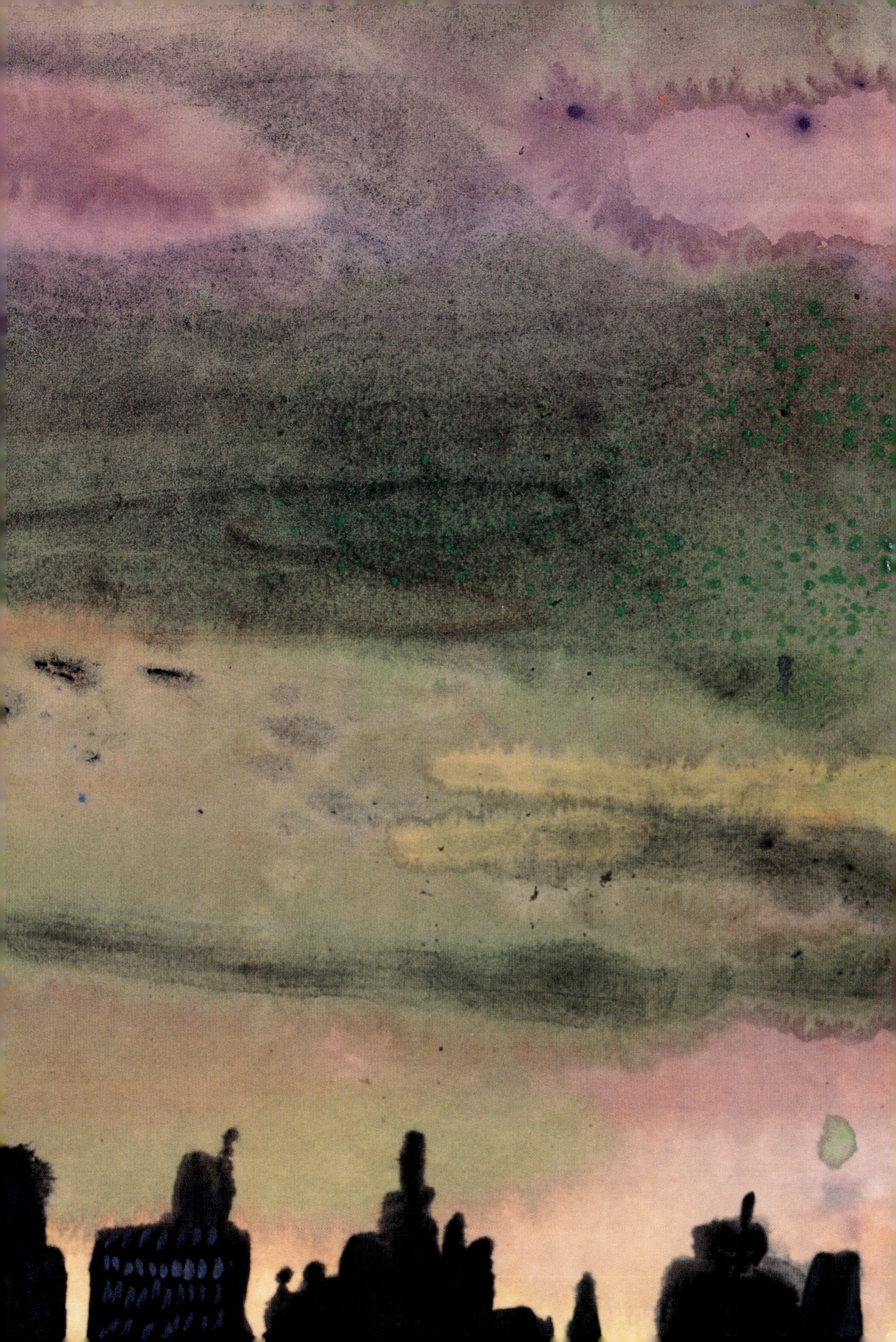

Everything driving everything
in a mad whirl
of depressed energy;
blank flicking of LEDs,
cutoffs.

*

Jeff Fort, leader of El Rukns
(Blackstone Rangers) street-voices
echo in my ear like ruin.
I haven't been to the pageantry of it;
she was more dissecting a means
of fucking around with the mind-set
of Fuctilig...Iowa.
Idaho, Les Halles. It's
all off to a foreign toy-
maker. And everything
she wears is plated in
silver. She smiles
and bangs the door.

*

General MacArthur battens,
aerobics instructor loosens
her hair, Roosevelt, first
thing in the morning, my
hair at an angle to the
wind. Is expunged at worst
as daylights' soggy weight
incurs lax sensitivity.
Tiny, flagrant bombs
go off during the onslaught,

prefiguring: "Grand Gladys
and the Phone Works." It's
2:47. They probably
fuck up your set.
I'm older and deader.

*

My life was so
endless. Sometimes
I wrote to no
one, nothing.
My eyes are always
shattered above
me, monitors'
great warmth fixes
in head above
bound systems, will
cherished, exploded,
faintly merry in
damp noon.

*

I'll be late
with those stories,
abridgement pink
wrapping, advent
lapis lazuli heart

everybody's fucked
of the war

*

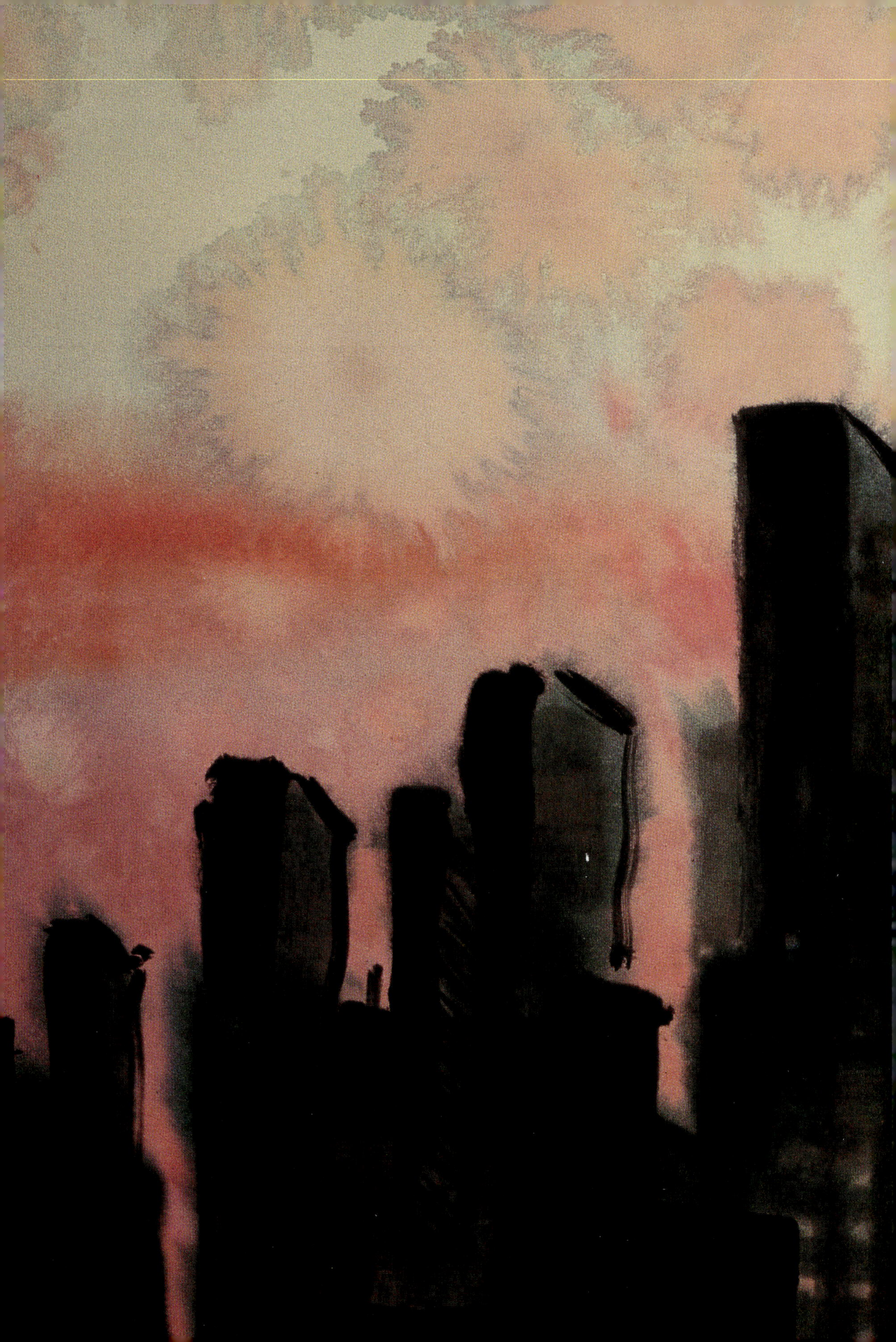

**Blow**

I'm not going to blow it this time
Though my step is treaded in error.

When I look at the wreck of my life
It all went wrong years ago.

I've poured out my heart to this city.
City's got to give something back soon.

# Vincent Katz

Vincent Katz is a poet, translator, and critic. He is the author of *Boulevard Transportation* (Tibor de Nagy Editions, 1997) and New York Hello! (Ommation Press, 1990), both with photographs by Rudy Burckhardt, *Cabal Of Zealots* (Hanuman Books, 1988), and *A Tremor In The Morning* (Peter Blum Edition, 1986, with linocuts by Alex Katz), all books of poetry. In 1995, he published *Charm* (Sun & Moon Press), a book of translations from Latin of the Roman love poet Sextus Propertius. His writing has appeared in *Aperture, Art in America, ARTnews, Flash Art, Interview,* and *Parkett.*

# Tabboo!

Tabboo!, real name Stephen Tashjian, is an Armenian-American, aquarian artist originally from Massachusetts where his paintings were recently installed at the Institute of Contemporary Art Museum in Boston. He lives in Manhattan and uses the colorful essence of New York City as the subject of his art exploring his own spiritual journey. Tabboo! has exhibited his paintings, drawings and performances as far north as Montreal, south as Miami Beach, west as Seattle, and east as Berlin. He is currently represented by Wooster Gardens Gallery, New York.

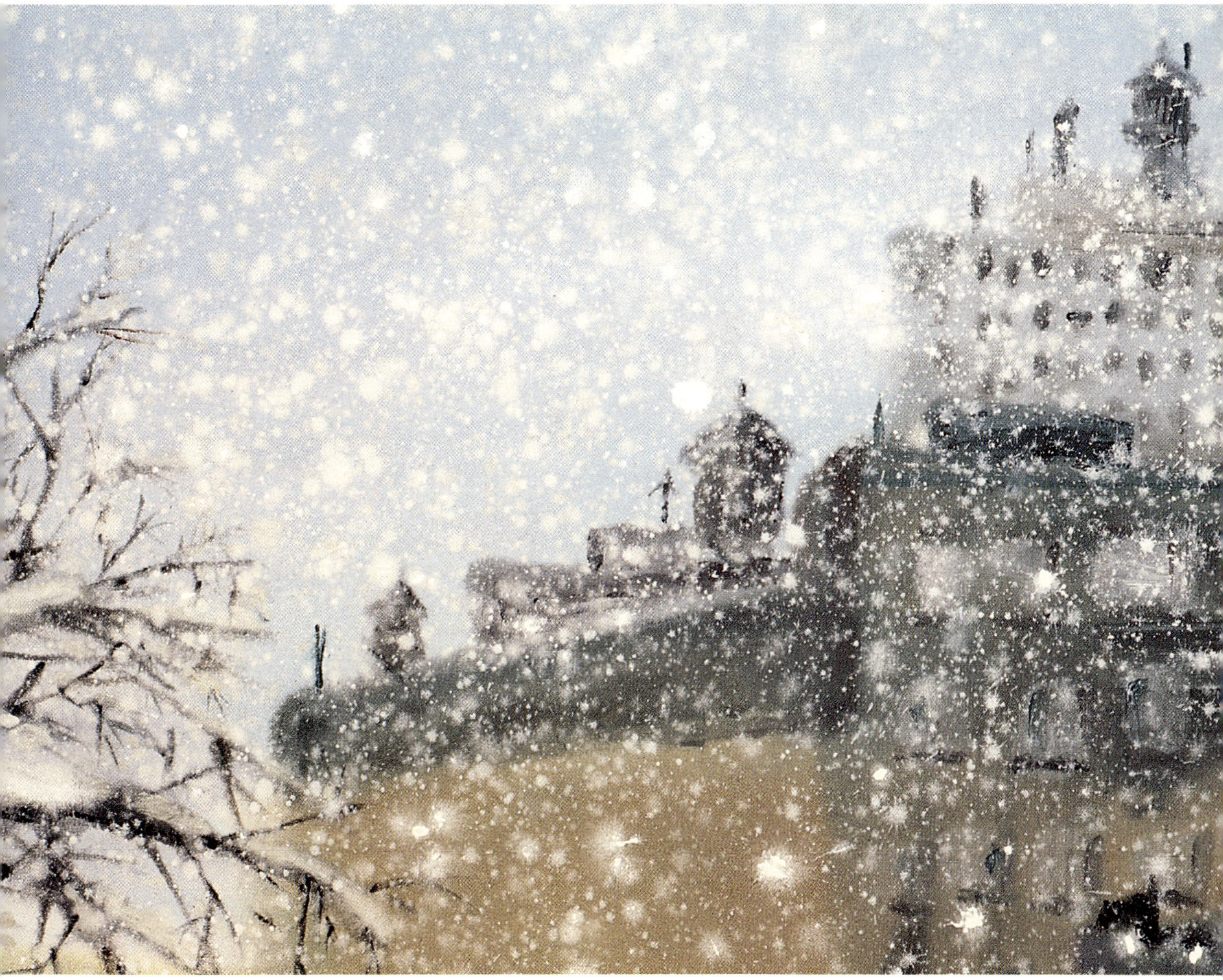

PEARL: Poems by Vincent Katz, Paintings by Tabboo!



"Pearl" was originally published in *Exquisite Corpse* issue #46 and "the 40th" in *The World* issue #



Published in the United States by powerHouse Books,
a division of powerHouse Cultural Entertainment, Inc.
180 Varick Street, Suite 1302, New York, NY 10014-4606
telephone 212 604 9074, fax 212 366 5247
e-mail: info@powerHouseBooks.com
web site: http://www.powerHouseBooks.com

First edition, 1998

Library of Congress Cataloging-in-Publication Data:

Tabboo!, 1959—
Pearl / art by Tabboo! ; poetry by Vincent Katz. -- 1st ed.
p. cm.
ISBN 1-57687-016-2
1. Tabboo!, 1959- --Themes, motives. 2. New York (N.Y.)--In art. I. Katz, Vincent, 1960- . II. Title.
ND237.T295A4 1998
759. 13--DC21 97-51307
CIP

ISBN 1-57687-016-2

Project coordination: Marcelo Cardoso
Four-color separations by: Job Color, Bergamo
Printed and bound by: L.E.G.O. Eurografica, Vicenza

A special deluxe edition of twelve original pieces, hand-painted by Tabboo! with hand-written wor
by Vincent Katz, were created for this book. Please inquire with the publisher.

A complete catalog of powerHouse Books and Limited Editions is
available upon request; please call, write, or hit our web site.

10 9 8 7 6 5 4 3 2 1

Printed and bound in Italy

Art direction by: Vivien Bittencourt
Book design by: Marcelo Cardoso
Hand lettering by: Tabboo!